72'

BOR SCORES 5

POPULAR PIANO SOLOS · BOOK 16

THIS PUBLICATION IS NOT AUTHORISED FOR SALE IN
THE UNITED STATES OF AMERICA AND/OR CANADA.

WISE PUBLICATIONS
LONDON/NEW YORK/PARIS/SYDNEY/COPENHAGEN/MADRID

EXCLUSIVE DISTRIBUTORS:
MUSIC SALES LIMITED
8/9 FRITH STREET,
LONDON W1V 5TZ, ENGLAND.

MUSIC SALES PTY LIMITED
120 ROTHSCHILD AVENUE,
ROSEBERY, NSW 2018,
AUSTRALIA.

THIS BOOK © COPYRIGHT 1996 BY WISE PUBLICATIONS
ORDER NO. AM937002
ISBN 0-7119-5748-7

MUSIC ARRANGED BY STEPHEN DURO
MUSIC PROCESSED BY ALLEGRO REPRODUCTIONS
COMPILED BY PETER EVANS
ORIGINAL BOOK DESIGN BY HOWARD BROWN
COVER BY PEARCE MARCHBANK, STUDIO TWENTY

MUSIC SALES' COMPLETE CATALOGUE DESCRIBES THOUSANDS OF TITLES
AND IS AVAILABLE IN FULL COLOUR SECTIONS BY SUBJECT,
DIRECT FROM MUSIC SALES LIMITED.
PLEASE STATE YOUR AREAS OF INTEREST AND
SEND A CHEQUE/POSTAL ORDER FOR £1.50 FOR POSTAGE TO:
MUSIC SALES LIMITED, NEWMARKET ROAD,
BURY ST. EDMUNDS, SUFFOLK IP33 3YB.

YOUR GUARANTEE OF QUALITY
AS PUBLISHERS, WE STRIVE TO PRODUCE EVERY BOOK
TO THE HIGHEST COMMERCIAL STANDARDS.
THE MUSIC HAS BEEN FRESHLY ENGRAVED AND THE BOOK HAS BEEN
CAREFULLY DESIGNED TO MINIMISE AWKWARD PAGE TURNS
AND TO MAKE PLAYING FROM IT A REAL PLEASURE.
PARTICULAR CARE HAS BEEN GIVEN TO SPECIFYING ACID-FREE,
NEUTRAL-SIZED PAPER MADE FROM PULPS WHICH HAVE NOT BEEN
ELEMENTAL CHLORINE BLEACHED. THIS PULP IS FROM FARMED
SUSTAINABLE FORESTS AND WAS PRODUCED WITH
SPECIAL REGARD FOR THE ENVIRONMENT.
THROUGHOUT, THE PRINTING AND BINDING HAVE BEEN PLANNED
TO ENSURE A STURDY, ATTRACTIVE PUBLICATION
WHICH SHOULD GIVE YEARS OF ENJOYMENT.
IF YOUR COPY FAILS TO MEET OUR HIGH STANDARDS,
PLEASE INFORM US AND WE WILL GLADLY REPLACE IT.

UNAUTHORISED REPRODUCTION OF ANY PART OF
THIS PUBLICATION BY ANY MEANS INCLUDING PHOTOCOPYING
IS AN INFRINGEMENT OF COPYRIGHT.

PRINTED IN THE UNITED KINGDOM BY
REDWOOD BOOKS, TROWBRIDGE, WILTSHIRE

HAMPSHIRE COUNTY LIBRARY

786.4 | 0711957487

C003384228

A TIME FOR US (LOVE THEME FROM ROMEO & JULIET)

MUSIC BY NINO ROTA
WORDS BY EDDIE SNYDER & LARRY KUSIK

© COPYRIGHT 1969 FAMOUS MUSIC CORPORATION, USA.
ALL RIGHTS RESERVED. INTERNATIONAL COPYRIGHT SECURED.

BEYOND THE BLUE HORIZON

WORDS & MUSIC BY LEO ROBIN, RICHARD WHITING & FRANKE W. HARLING

Moderately

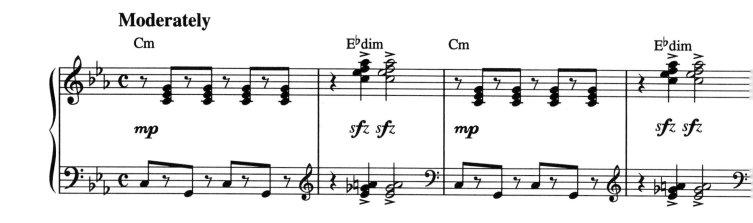

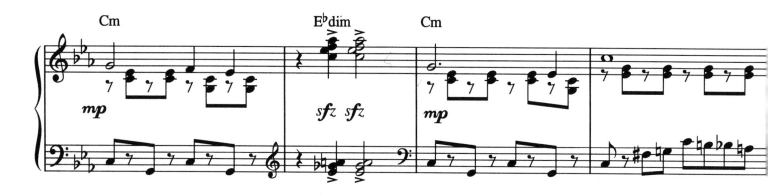

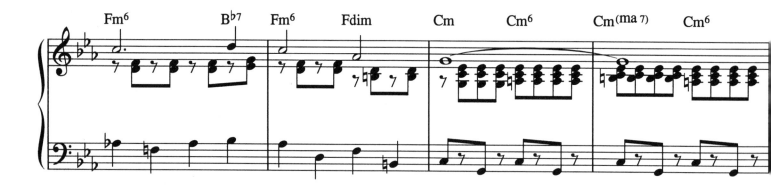

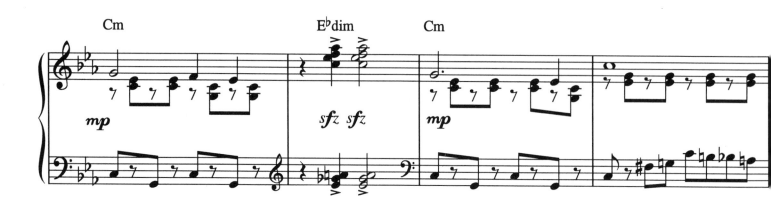

© COPYRIGHT 1930 FAMOUS MUSIC CORPORATION, USA.
ALL RIGHTS RESERVED. INTERNATIONAL COPYRIGHT SECURED.

7

CHELSEA BRIDGE

BY BILLY STRAYHORN

© COPYRIGHT 1942 TEMPO MUSIC INCORPORATED, USA.
CAMPBELL CONNELLY & COMPANY LIMITED, 8/9 FRITH STREET, LONDON W1.
ALL RIGHTS RESERVED. INTERNATIONAL COPYRIGHT SECURED.

DO YOU KNOW THE WAY TO SAN JOSE

WORDS BY HAL DAVID
MUSIC BY BURT BACHARACH

Moderately, rhythmically

© COPYRIGHT 1967 & 1968 NEW HIDDEN VALLEY MUSIC COMPANY AND JAC MUSIC COMPANY INCORPORATED, USA.
MCA MUSIC LIMITED, 77 FULHAM PALACE ROAD, LONDON W6 (50%)/
WINDSWEPT PACIFIC MUSIC LIMITED, 27 QUEENSDALE PLACE, LONDON W11 (50%).
ALL RIGHTS RESERVED. INTERNATIONAL COPYRIGHT SECURED.

FOR ALL WE KNOW

WORDS BY ROBB WILSON & ARTHUR JAMES
MUSIC BY FRED KARLIN

© COPYRIGHT 1970 BY PAMCO MUSIC INCORPORATED, USA.
© COPYRIGHT 1971 BY AMPA MUSIC CORPORATION, USA.
MCA MUSIC LIMITED, 77 FULHAM PALACE ROAD, LONDON W6.
ALL RIGHTS RESERVED. INTERNATIONAL COPYRIGHT SECURED.

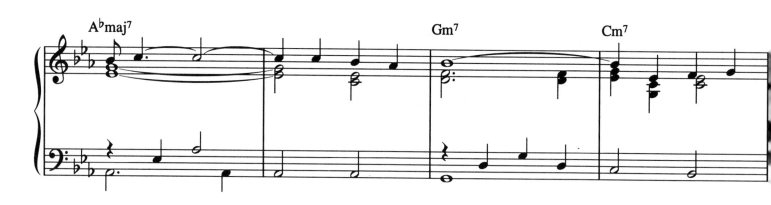

A♭maj⁷ Gm⁷ Cm⁷

A♭maj⁷ B♭⁷sus E♭ *D.S. al Coda*

⊕ *CODA*

Gm⁷ Cm⁷ A♭maj⁷

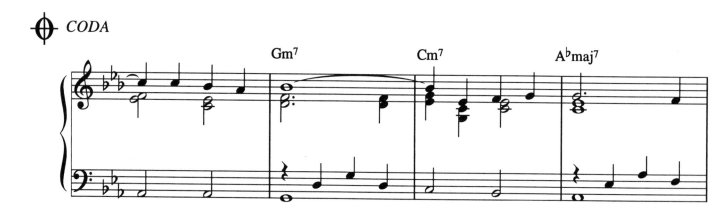

B♭⁷sus E♭

rit.

pp

HERE'S THAT RAINY DAY

WORDS & MUSIC BY JOHNNY BURKE & JIMMY VAN HEUSEN

© COPYRIGHT 1953 BURKE & VAN HEUSEN INCORPORATED.
ALL RIGHTS ASSIGNED TO BOURNE COMPANY & DORSEY BROTHERS MUSIC INCORPORATED.
WARNER CHAPPELL MUSIC LIMITED, 129 PARK STREET, LONDON W1 (50%)/
CAMPBELL CONNELLY & COMPANY LIMITED, 8/9 FRITH STREET, LONDON W1 (50%).
ALL RIGHTS RESERVED. INTERNATIONAL COPYRIGHT SECURED.

I DON'T WANT TO WALK WITHOUT YOU

MUSIC BY JULE STYNE
WORDS BY FRANK LOESSER

© COPYRIGHT 1942 PARAMOUNT MUSIC CORPORATION & FAMOUS MUSIC CORPORATION, USA.
ALL RIGHTS RESERVED. INTERNATIONAL COPYRIGHT SECURED.

IN THE COOL, COOL, COOL OF THE EVENING

MUSIC BY HOAGY CARMICHAEL
WORDS BY JOHNNY MERCER

© COPYRIGHT 1951 FAMOUS MUSIC CORPORATION, USA.
ALL RIGHTS RESERVED. INTERNATIONAL COPYRIGHT SECURED.

I'M GETTIN' SENTIMENTAL OVER YOU

WORDS BY NED WASHINGTON
MUSIC BY GEO. BASSMAN

© COPYRIGHT 1933 LAWRENCE MUSIC PUBLISHERS INCORPORATED, USA.
© COPYRIGHT ASSIGNED 1934 MILLS MUSIC INCORPORATED, USA.
DASH MUSIC COMPANY LIMITED, 8/9 FRITH STREET, LONDON W1.
ALL RIGHTS RESERVED. INTERNATIONAL COPYRIGHT SECURED.

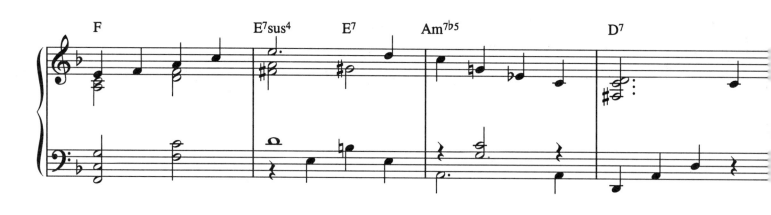

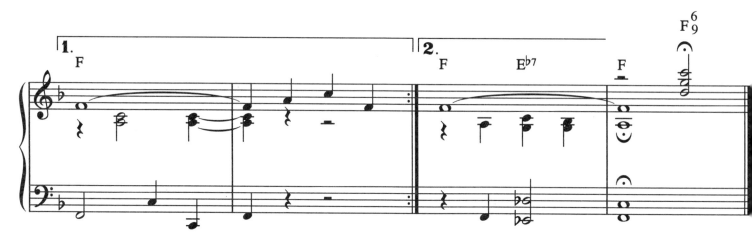

IT COULD HAPPEN TO YOU

MUSIC BY JIMMY VAN HEUSEN
WORDS BY JOHNNY BURKE

© COPYRIGHT 1944 FAMOUS MUSIC CORPORATION, USA.
ALL RIGHTS RESERVED. INTERNATIONAL COPYRIGHT SECURED.

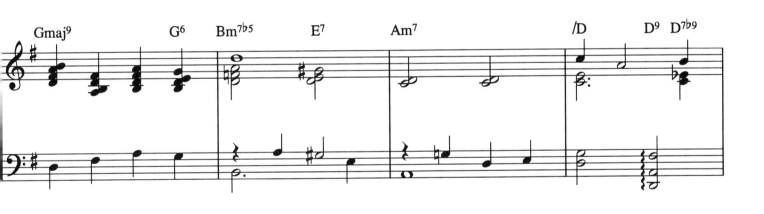

LOVER

MUSIC BY RICHARD RODGERS
WORDS BY LORENZ HART

© COPYRIGHT 1932 FAMOUS MUSIC CORPORATION, USA.
ALL RIGHTS RESERVED. INTERNATIONAL COPYRIGHT SECURED.

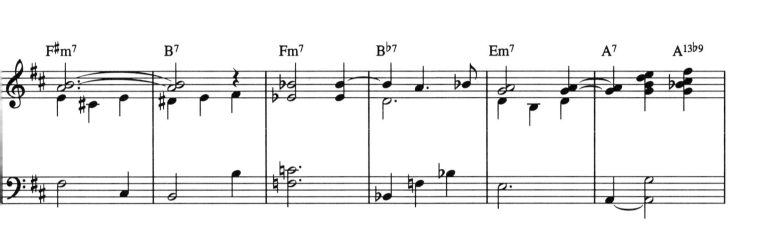

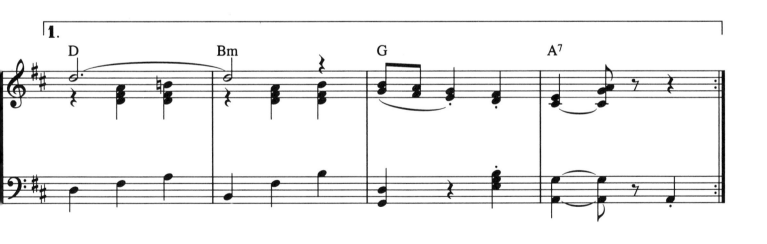

MONA LISA

WORDS & MUSIC BY JAY LIVINGSTON & RAY EVANS

© COPYRIGHT 1949 FAMOUS MUSIC CORPORATION, USA.
ALL RIGHTS RESERVED. INTERNATIONAL COPYRIGHT SECURED.

MOONLIGHT BECOMES YOU

MUSIC BY JIMMY VAN HEUSEN
WORDS BY JOHNNY BURKE

© COPYRIGHT 1942 FAMOUS MUSIC CORPORATION, USA.
ALL RIGHTS RESERVED. INTERNATIONAL COPYRIGHT SECURED.

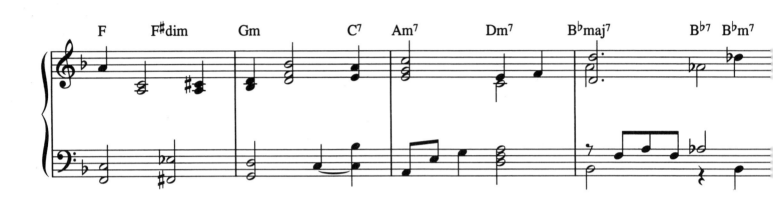

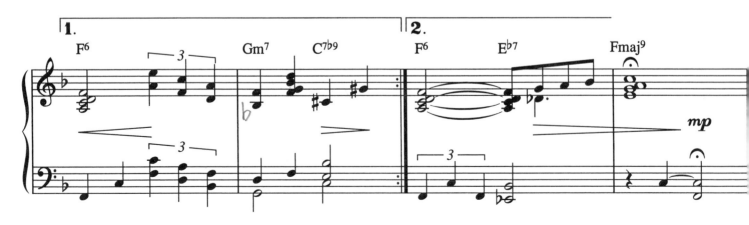

MY OLD FLAME

WORDS & MUSIC BY ARTHUR JOHNSTON & SAM COSLOW

© COPYRIGHT 1934 PARAMOUNT MUSIC CORPORATION & FAMOUS MUSIC CORPORATION, USA.
ALL RIGHTS RESERVED. INTERNATIONAL COPYRIGHT SECURED.

ON A SLOW BOAT TO CHINA

WORDS & MUSIC BY FRANK LOESSER

Moderately with a beat

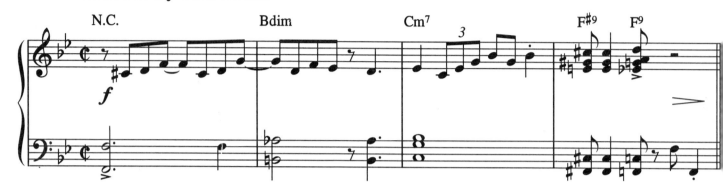

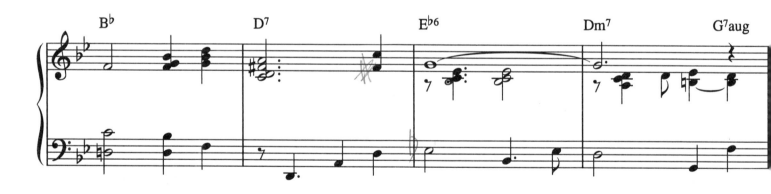

© COPYRIGHT 1948 BY FRANK MUSIC CORPORATION, USA. RENEWED 1976 FRANK MUSIC
CORPORATION, USA.
PUBLISHED & ADMINISTERED BY MPL COMMUNICATIONS LIMITED.
ALL RIGHTS RESERVED. INTERNATIONAL COPYRIGHT SECURED.

45

OUR DAY WILL COME

MUSIC BY BOB HILLIARD
WORDS BY MORT GARSON

Moderately slow

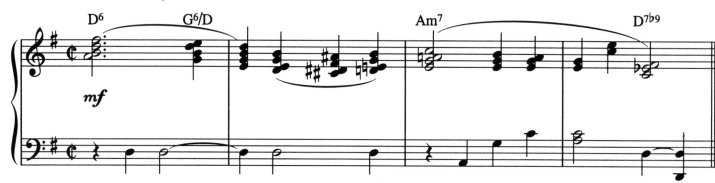

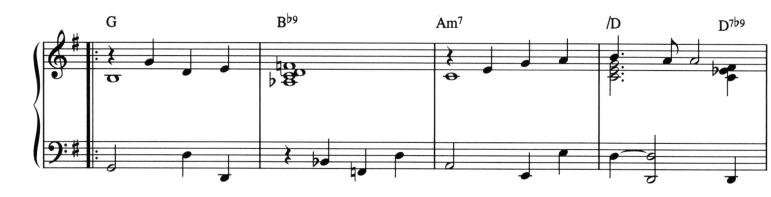

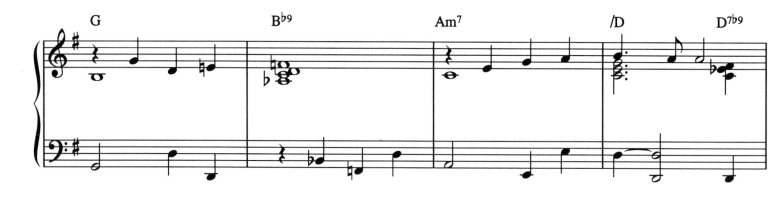

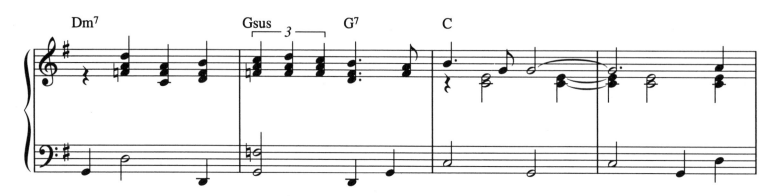

© COPYRIGHT 1963 BETTER HALF MUSIC COMPANY, USA.
MCA MUSIC LIMITED, 77 FULHAM PALACE ROAD, LONDON W6. (50%)/
BOURNE MUSIC LIMITED, STANDBROOK HOUSE, 2-5 OLD BOND STREET, LONDON W1 (50%).
ALL RIGHTS RESERVED. INTERNATIONAL COPYRIGHT SECURED.

PRELUDE TO A KISS

WORDS & MUSIC BY DUKE ELLINGTON, IRVING GORDON & IRVING MILLS

© COPYRIGHT 1938 AMERICAN ACADEMY OF MUSIC INCORPORATED, USA.
AUTHORISED FOR SALE IN THE UK ONLY BY THE PERMISSION OF THE SOLE AGENTS, J.R. LAFLEUR & SON LIMITED.
ALL RIGHTS RESERVED. INTERNATIONAL COPYRIGHT SECURED.

49

SPEAK SOFTLY LOVE

MUSIC BY NINO ROTA
WORDS BY LARRY KUSIK

© COPYRIGHT 1972 FAMOUS MUSIC CORPORATION, USA.
ALL RIGHTS RESERVED. INTERNATIONAL COPYRIGHT SECURED.

TAKE MY BREATH AWAY

WORDS BY TOM WHITLOCK
MUSIC BY GIORGIO MORODER

© COPYRIGHT 1986 GIORGIO MORODER PUBLISHING COMPANY & FAMOUS MUSIC CORPORATION, USA.
ALL RIGHTS RESERVED. INTERNATIONAL COPYRIGHT SECURED.

THAT OLD BLACK MAGIC

MUSIC BY HAROLD ARLEN
WORDS BY JOHNNY MERCER

Moderately bright

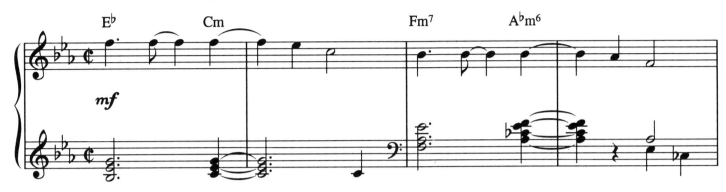

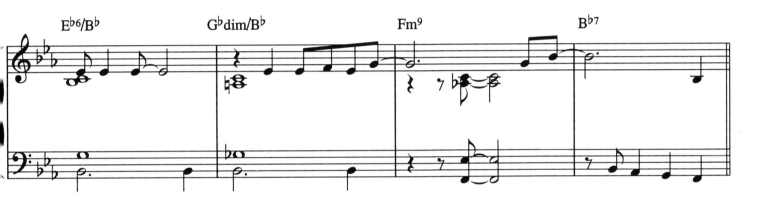

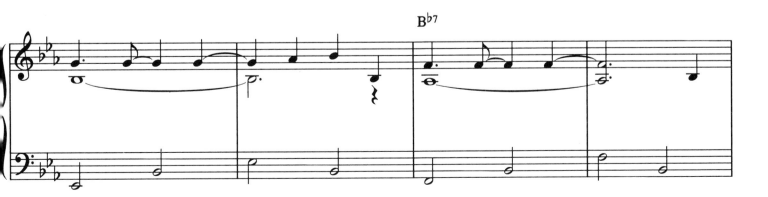

© COPYRIGHT 1942 FAMOUS MUSIC CORPORATION, USA.
ALL RIGHTS RESERVED. INTERNATIONAL COPYRIGHT SECURED.

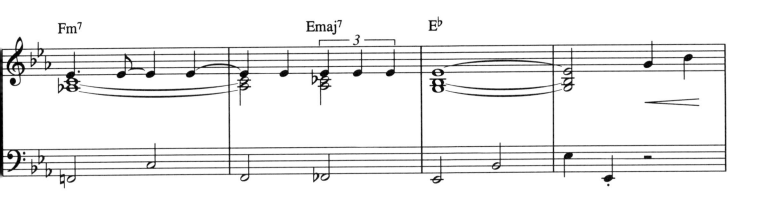

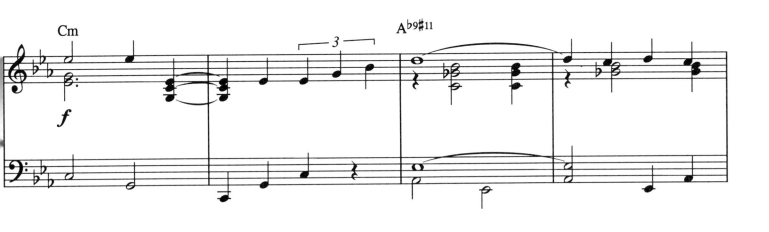

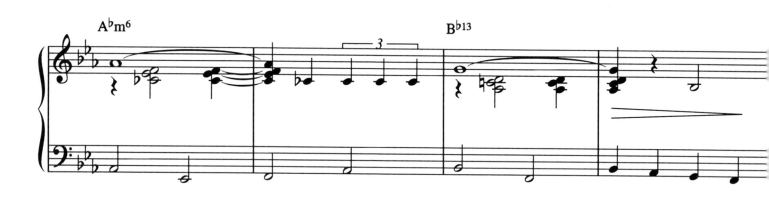

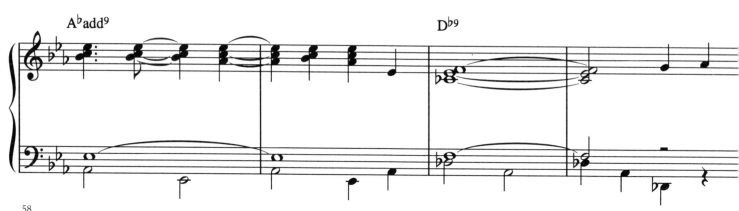

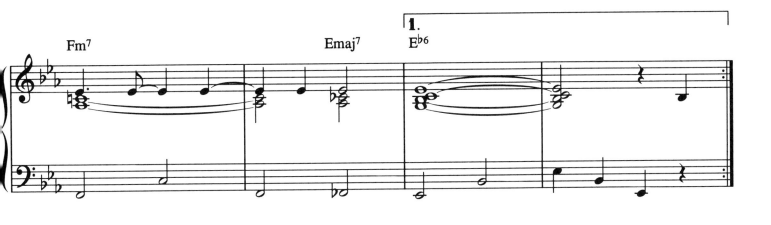

WISH ME A RAINBOW

WORDS & MUSIC BY JERRY LIVINGSTON & RAY EVANS

© COPYRIGHT 1966 FAMOUS MUSIC CORPORATION, USA.
ALL RIGHTS RESERVED. INTERNATIONAL COPYRIGHT SECURED.

61

THE NEARNESS OF YOU

MUSIC BY HOAGY CARMICHAEL
WORDS BY NED WASHINGTON

© COPYRIGHT 1937, 1940 RENEWED 1964, 1967 FAMOUS MUSIC CORPORATION, USA.
ALL RIGHTS RESERVED. INTERNATIONAL COPYRIGHT SECURED.